Poems from the Black Sea

~~~~~~~~~~~~~~~~~
~~~~~~~~~~~~~~~~~

Denis Knight was born in Volo, Greece, and lived as a boy in Trébizond, on the Black Sea. Educated in England at St. Edmund's College, Ware, and at Christ's College, Cambridge. Served with the 44th Bn. Royal Tank Regiment, in North Africa and Europe between 1941 and 1945. This was his most basic education. Married to Nora Dalton in 1942. She paints. Four sons, one daughter. These, with his grandchildren, were his further education.

The author at 21

Poems from the Black Sea

An Anthology
Denis Knight

Writer's Showcase
presented by *Writer's Digest*
San Jose New York Lincoln Shanghai

Acknowledgements

Acknowledgements are due to Dorothy Day, Editor of the *The Catholic Worker*, N.Y., where five of these poems were first published; to Walter Lowenfels, who edited *Where is Vietnam? American Poets Respond* (Doubleday Anchor Original, N.Y.) for 'Schoolday in Man Quang'; to *Peace News*, London, for 'The Bridge' and 'Alice Says No'; to *The New Statesman*, London, for 'A Warning'; *to London Labour Briefing* for 'Twelve Police Horses'; to Jon Silkin, Editor of *Stand Magazine*, Newcastle upon Tyne, for eight poems from Occitania, France.

Contents

Sweet Felpham

No dust had gathered on the floors of paradise,
Not a tile loose in the whole roof of heaven,
Nor single spider in the bath of the immortals,
No washing-up to do. Not a missing cup or saucer.
But in the garden poppies, sunflowers, cornflowers, marigolds.

She sits so beautiful with her baby daughter.
Two boys run races to the battered blue gate.

"The Bread of sweet Thought & the Wine of Delight
Feeds the Village of Felpham by day and by night," said William Blake.

The Black Sea

Today I come from Trebizond to sell
As much as your imagination buys
Of eucalyptus leaf and bark and smell.
Under the broken water-jar remark
The implacable scorpion sitting in the dark.
Or watch him on the wall, part of the stone
The lizard gently swallowing in the sun.

Where clusters of the grape too high
For Dounia's hands to reach
Hang in luxury from the sky
With pomegranate, peach
A fountain glistens in four children's eyes~
Fragments of rainbow memories~
And in that Turkish summer, through rusted iron spout
The sweet waters of Asia trickle out
To slip by tiny falls and processes
Down through the blazing lemon terraces
Into the dark at last, the black and bottled sea.

Days Like Trees

The only traveller is man moving through time
Square static hours like fields
Time of the sudden landscape motionless
Who sees the dark upstanding days like trees
And the dark horizons of the centuries.

Time flies? Not time that flies but man who swings
Idly between the poles of past and future
Bewildered by the softness of his flight
Never accustomed to the use of wings.

River Common

You came, Edward Thomas, to an end of forest
And felt the light, and smelt the drying grass
And found yourself another self beyond your trees.

I came today to the top of River Common
And delighted in the straight sunlight.
She swung open the new gate, leading to a clear way

Smooth-trod by children through the bracken,
Down the most sunlit hillside in England,
Home.

Hiroshima

The last petal from the last flower
Falls like a sledgehammer in the world's garden.
The last petal from the last flower.

The last wind that blows on the last city
Blows into nothing women, men.
The last wind on the last city.

The last man back from the last shore-party
Expects the hurricane.
I am that man. You too are he.

The Desert and the Flood

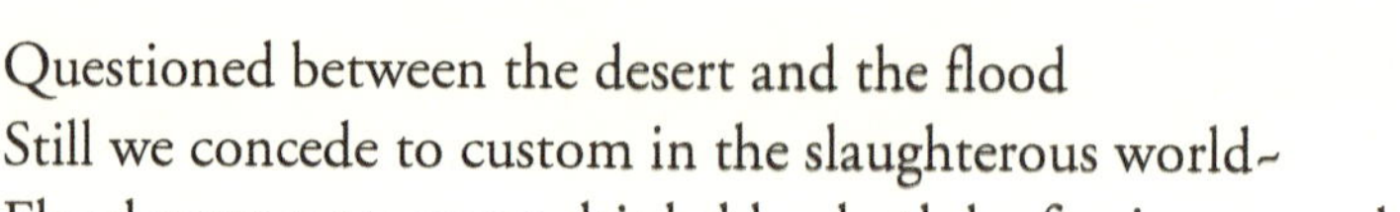

Questioned between the desert and the flood
Still we concede to custom in the slaughterous world~
Floodwater soon seems drinkable, death by famine normal,
The breaking of the sun acceptable.

Questioned between the firestorm and the flood
Still we concede to beauty in the barbarous world~
Pieces of happened beauty indisputable.
Under the bombs, I saw her comb her hair.

Questioned between the desert and the flood
Still am I slain by beauty in the merciful world~
The leaf of olive held up still in the dove's beak:
Her hands, her fearless eyes, her bodily truth.

Let Not Those Kind F-Words Be Lost

All lost?
The heroes dead?
Troy gate swings useless on its post
Where Hector in full sun
Fell, while his blood played and shone.

Though Troy crack, seven walls burn,
Let not those words be lost
Which Paris, lacking Greek,
Fumbled into Helen's breast
While worlds grew warm.

Let not those kind F-words be lost
Of Aubrey Cullum at Primasole Bridge:
Of my friend Hugh Bishop on the Sangro
Delicately shrapnel-wounded in the tank, soon dead.
Ken Sinden, serious drinker, young Robin Anderson
The Scot, companions brewing merrily in petrol-engined
Sherman tank, in Normandy, July, Hill One-One-Two.
Jack Thorogood at St Oedenrode; Len Williams
Joking, wounded, pipe in hand, with Benny Shaw.
"No word of theirs is lost," the padre hazarded.
"No lie unsaid," they laughing all replied.

In tribute to the 230 men, mostly Bristolians, of the 44th Royal Tank Regiment ('Black Desert Rats') killed in North Africa and Europe, 1941–45.

Walking in the New World

I am walking in the new world, Nora
Come walk with me in Canada.

Stars over eyes
Snow at your feet
The warm tree stands between.

You know of course that stars are made of snow
And snow of stars?
And all is one and one is good?
I know that too.

Where is the shadow of the moon upon the sun?
Where is the dark?
Where is the dark tonight
When all is one, and one is lost in light?

When all is snow and stars, and dark is bright?
No end no end to such a kiss, my wife
No end, no end, but new world spinning bright

No shadow, alteration, end. All light, all life.

The Loyalist Burial-Ground

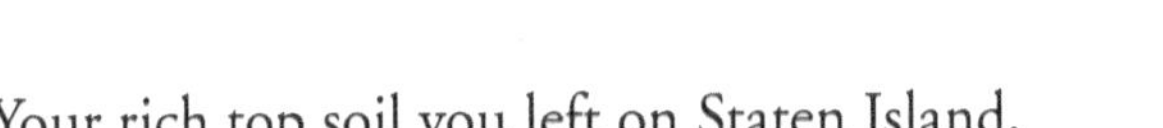

Your rich top soil you left on Staten Island,
White house with slaves and horses, patrimony;
And in small indignant ships
Fled for New Brunswick rock and bitter fir.

Stout squire and his imperious, timid lady
Berthed by the Upper Cove, Saint John,
Extended loyal foot on royal rock,
Mostly died young and dug themselves neat graves
(Some with iron railings, English county fashion)
Beneath the small maples in the Loyalist Burial-ground,
Each headstone meticulously engraved.

Dying seems at first what they did best.
Then farming cautiously along the creeks of the Saint John
American-wise in the blueberry meadows where cow
Milked well enough in June, corn suddenly shot
In the violent July sun, the brown hen laid,
And all went well. Deep from the heart of cedar
Under snow her sons pulled whaling-ships,
Her daughters learned to spin-though Grandmamma in May
Allowed herself the faintest, feathered sigh
Remembering Massachusetts, Connecticut, Vermont,
The earlier flowers and milder trees of home.

St Dionysus, Martyr

God loves all existing things, said Thomas Aquinas.

Never seek any happiness in earth, or heaven.
Only, when you are in heaven, have the sense to recognize it.

I will tell you for nothing where heaven is~
All you philosophers who enquire
Of publicans and saints who smelt and handled it.

Heaven is in the eating of three slim sardines
From Norway, Canada, Galilee
With a few small onions raw from the market
Of Saint John, N B,
Asleep in oil of olives upon wheaten bread.

O seventh-heaven Paul,
Augustine now chaste, cold
Dominic, and golden beggar of Assisi~
And you my martyrs Rusticus & Eleutherius, Dionysus!
Heaven is in the eating of bread, and fish, and oil,
And a little red wine from the bottom of the bottle,
And knowing that these are good, and will stay good
Under Fundy Bay and in the earth and in the sun,
O my Dionysus, martyr perpetual,
Hungering and thirsting after truth and justice
Even in pleasant heaven.

Perhaps We Have Won

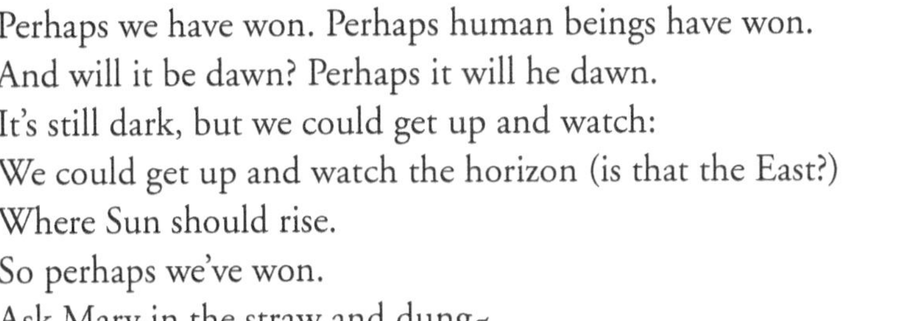

Perhaps we have won. Perhaps human beings have won.
And will it be dawn? Perhaps it will he dawn.
It's still dark, but we could get up and watch:
We could get up and watch the horizon (is that the East?)
Where Sun should rise.
So perhaps we've won.
Ask Mary in the straw and dung~
She'll know about the milk and winding-sheet, cot, and tombstone.

But listen. This is urgent:
There is a rubbish-heap beyond the City
On a bit of hill outside the City,
And within that Golgotha a viable seed
A mustard-seed to burn the heart and tongue.
The seed takes root (the story will end well?)
And shoots up branches, leaves, and nightingales.
Now Socrates one bitter night stops by the tree,
And never moves till dawn, thinking what Crito said.
Sophocles too stands there and in the Athenian night
Listens to words truthful Antigone spoke
Among the shards and rubbish of that place
Where the body of her noble brother lies unburied.

This rubbish-heap is Sion, Holy Mountain, everlasting
Calvary height on height.
And Socrates, Sophocles, Gautama and the rest
Look up, look up at branches how they spread
In cross symmetrical, quartering the universe
Men mar, God makes.
We should get up, though it's still dark, and wait.
Shall the Child bring victory this Christmas?
Shall the Man bring victory this Easter?

All These People

———— ∞ ————

All these people wandering about in the world
Are flowers hand-sown, transplanted:
Leaves in the sun: roots in water, minerals, muck.
All these people wandering about in the world
Who smile, who sigh, stand up, get blown down,

Are free beyond the careful gardener's question.
The cloud moves back and forth across the sun,
Wide world rolls over and over joyfully:
In fire of heart, in flood of tears
His plants are scorched and drowned alternately.

He waits for best and worst, like every gardener.
Makes sure at least that strain of seed is true,
That men of yes and no stay fallible, free:
Put forth own roots, own shoots, own bud, own flower
In garden, vineyard, swamp-land, wilderness.

He sees indeed the fruit of the January tree,
And harvest moon in Vernal equinox:
Sees blossom, blight, crop bountiful: rejoices,
Grieves. But grafts again and again free men
On tree of perfect Liberty, on Christ.

Ninth Symphony

There was nobody, none
There was utterly no one
To whom Beethoven could speak

Nor did he speak but to the swaddled future
To put a match to fires as yet undreamed, unlit.
But sang in darkness

(Men called him deaf, unwived)
Eight songs of gladness
And ninth song glorious.

The Apple Orchard

A man's best actions have the wind and sun
Beating and burning round his mouth and eyes.
His every real action is a public one
Taken in the city, under dangerous skies.
Even his umbrella attracts the lightning.

But love is on the southern slope of the ridge,
And draws the tranquil heart in safety to it.
Here is your apple orchard in a double hedge
Of holly pointed to keep farm-traffic out.
From this deep ground men's greenest actions spring.

Martha and Mary

Christ in the house of Martha and Mary~
By Velasquez, in the National Gallery.

Someone's helping Martha in the kitchen get supper.
The Guest is seated in an inner room, talking with Mary.
Things needed for the meal are on the kitchen table:
Glazed green jug, for oil; red peppers, bits of garlic.
Four fish with brilliant eyes, fresh from salt-water.
In Martha's hand the solid pestle is lifted
To pound away those mysteries that lurk in the dark mortar:
Fish in this house are eaten without miracle.
Bread's for the children, not the tabernacle.

Martha's hands make every prompt decision,
Crack nuts, gut fish, make up the necessary bed
That spoils then heals his body in her own.
Her limbs choose no philosophies of good
But turn and rest at point of subtlest balance
Of earth's axis, and her husband's eyes.

Her sister Mary, miniatured in the inner room,
Hands clasped together still in yesterday's dream,
Consumes the future. The courteous Visitor,
Seeing that Mary's need is indeed greater,
Reassures her with kind words; and goes to Martha's supper.

Two Young Men at a Humble Table

Two young men eating at a humble table~
By Velasquez~painted when he was twenty.
Dark table, pestle, mortar, pot and jug.

Deep, companionable, abstracted conversation.
Secure on the neck of the earthenware pot
A peach, soft glowing, round peach with subtle leaf

Has made both men feel thirst of life for ever.
Which then will take it first? They both pretend
It isn't there. Each dares himself to steal

Her love, tonight. Tonight I'll dare.

Every Green Leaf

Today, tomorrow, or after his glad death
The poet will put back every green leaf

On each tree felled, defoliate, burned.
To every woman he will make return

Of the word most beautiful in her womb
That sings in mouth of girl, boy, woman, man.

And to the sun give back each word on fire
Struck from this communication pure.

'Field Work'

His verse had life in it very old
Before Seamus Heaney wrote it down.

It was lying on the road in blue
Limestone slab, peat-stench curled for none

But his hands to gloss, cradle, pick and cup
In this new-rain, gleaming, patient book.

Field Work, Seamus Heaney, 1979

Robert Graves

When old poet dies,~Sam Johnson in bed
Mumbling of Tetty, still urgently beloved,
With only Hodge present, his 'very fine' cat,
The venerable physician arriving late~
She whom he loved will not let go her hand
As poet saunters through a lasting land.

Rigged out for feast-day in cordobes hat,
Dark bardic cloak, ashplant, and red cravat,
Bury him coolly on his apple island
By carob tree, in olive-terraced valley.
His 'dance of words', though Robert Graves is dead,
'Begins in lightning and ends not' he said.

The Flint Knife

I now write
with this flint knife
broken words
my stone age brother
shaped with his finger
and left on the Down
for the wind to decipher.

Nora, Aquarius

This woman is a measure
Of the river.
She flows, she tumbles
Through the mill-house of her children.

She weaves the rainbow in the water-mill.
She dashes through tight places.
She the measure is
And measurer of her valley.

She floods meadows in summer.
After nights of thunder
Carries the dry water-course by storm.
She is conducive to lightning.

The sun-stripped Tréboulou
Irradiates and quantifies the valley.
She is source, aquifer, white water.
Rain-making and unmaking.

She is river looping and meandering.
In sun she on her lucid stream
Bears men. She flows
On silken skin, her clear eyes open.

Before You Get to Owley

She said, Before you get to Owley
Turn left by the ash for Ugber Beacon.

Cross Owley bridge where the Glaze brook sings,
Climb Owley hill by Owley cottage, then toil a mile

By hawthorn, ivy and stone-splitting oak
To the granite wall and bracken-line

That marks the kingdom of the mountain sheep
Unhedged, unfenced. Beyond the bracken waste

Sweet-nibbled grasses come, great stones lie down,
Windwoven thorns stand on the granite

To the Atlantic hardly bending,
Fastened in air, not growing not dying.

Under the sun's eye and the buzzard's
The white ram stands between the attentive ewes

Where Ugber granite sleeps its millioned years. These
Skyworn stones, she said, remember mountain ranges.

Orion Will Be Hunted

The wind stirs slightly in the holly leaves.
They stiffen, rustle: now the branch gives
Frightening the starlings from the chimney-pot.

Millions of stars are on the march tonight
Around the Pole, led by the Bear. Be sure
Tonight, next Moon, or in the Great Year

Orion will be hunted across the sky
By no strong gods, but by his weakest prey:
By millions of peaceful animals,

Birds, insects, fish, abounding whales
Species by species, swift nation by nation
With hardly a glance in our direction.

The Potter of Aujols

Truth bears a lovelier form than even
The potter can imagine for his pot,
Searching the valley and the mountain
With heart, with hand, with eyes that seek the truth.
The first maker of miraculous pots
Shattered himself to throw the pot refined
In fire of truth that would outlast mankind.
We break ourselves, before we break our pots.

Men now are potters labouring to fire
Pots of much greater beauty than themselves.
These pots assume magnificence, the power
Of heavenly bodies, gods and goddesses
Casting huge shadows from the sun, moon, stars
Eclipsing earth, us human creatures.

Magic, My Cat

Magic, my cat, won't let me read
Seeing Things, by Seamus Heaney
From Faber & Faber, paperback.

My cat sees things as they feel.
Sits on the whiteness of the book.
Steps on consonant and vowel.

A book is just white paper, says my cat~
Though poet puts strange marks on it.
It makes a comfortable place

To lick thoughts clean, sharpen claws.
Say what you will of bards and seers,
We cats make the true philosophers.

The Number 3 Bus

The Number 3 bus to Sandymount.
Here Ireland looks at Wales,
Washes the same white shells.

A man leads an old dog, blind:
It's sniffing the seaweed.
The tide is out. Somewhere on this strand

Joyce met with beauty unconsidered
For ever and for ever.
A seabird's cry. I think of her

In Keswick church arriving late for mass,
Who lifted up her heart to me
At the tide's full race.

A Certain Hillside

———— ∞ ————

"…and blessed is he," an apple
to hand, on a meadow hill
over Brent, under Dartmoor.
In the rowan tree's shade sharpens his scythe
two slim sickles and George Pratt's
worn down fagging-hook from River Common.
At the tree's foot the whetstone
and full bucket from the well,
on this south-sloping plat
in sheep meadow, at Splatton,
on Hazel Land, under Brent Hill and old Beara Common.

…and blessed is he who before he dies
handles his newly spitten and sharp blade
to a dawn purpose on a dew-wet hillside
on one planet anciently and newly blessed
through some coincidence~as thought Lucretius~
of particles of light in an embrace
with generous Time and generous Space
to form by generous Chance, seeds
of things greater than themselves:
sow-thistle, vetch and ryegrasses, cocksfoot run wild,
seeds of white clover, strong plantains, nettles by
fence and tumbling meadowsweet, milk-white starry things.
These scythe through my body,
sweep up my heart.

The bee in the thistle,
ourselves on this planet.
Looked at like this
a word is a different kind of grass.
All is at peace, though suns collapse.

"Sing Openly!"

Driving by accident to the guillotine
Diana huntress came this darkened way
Dear "ultimate rebel" joyful, complex, simple

And everywhere the people's queen of hearts
But to complete "these dear, unfinished tasks of mine"
Aids, lepers, landmines and sick children

She from her flowering gun-carriage cries out
"Sing openly! Sing openly, all you people there!
Sing openly, my William! and my Harry!"

Falling and Getting Up

'I'm a bit broken!'
Says she, at last, fourteen
Days afterwards, when
Nora from the attic ladder
Flew down backwards to the windowsill,
Then headlong halfway down the cottage stairs.

I thought of her in nineteen-fifty-something
With three children in the ponytrap from Upperton
(Baby at home in cot) dashing at a smart trot through
Pheasant Copse from River Common with the sun
Just up, to catch the bus at Petworth for the school
In Midhurst~and all her life not used to falling.

From over forty years ago, I catch again
That dreamday on the Common in October when
I fell with her 'slow motion' to the orchard grass,
The apple-tree around me, its laden branches
Folding me as the whole tree collapsed,
All its ripe apples on it.

Old George Wadey,
Commoner and peasant farmer on Pitts Hill,
Had never in his life on River Common
Witnessed a laden apple-tree fall thus
Grandly to the grass, the apple-picker in it.
How Wadey smiled, amazed, was silent, thoughtful.

Now, after these swiftly tumbling years
Of falling, getting up, crossing the Atlantic
In 'the heaviest seas for thirty years' on the Arkadia
Here is my Nora coming back this April morning
Calmly to her loving, active land of doing,
Painting her clear vision of real things,
Her music of events, sweet years in France, in Occitania
And now in Brent, between the Hill and Ougbeare Beacon.

What Are They?

What is poetry?
It is the earth
Speaking to itself
And understanding

And what is music?
It is the earth
Singing to itself
And listening

Piboulède

New Moon, Old Sun

New moon, old sun, Vega and starry chance
All have swirled round to pull us into this
Unlikely rendezvous in time, motion, space~
A wooden bed, in a house of stone, in France.

La Chasse

In France the faint dawn-chorus falls and rises
Somewhere between her hair and eyelashes.
The birds seek refuge in this tangled space
Away from juniper, burnt hedges, and 'la chasse'.

Two Things, Said Noë Marty

Two things, said Noë Marty ("Paysan je suis!")
Two things made Piboulède a village~
And every other village on the Causse.
First, the spring, 'la source' at its secret
Opening in the limestone bedrock,
An aquifer gone astray, drawn to the sky.
Here stand his 'piboules', poplars, roots near water:
This mud was once a pond for sheep and oxen.
At the spring's head, all brambles now, hewn
Stones to keep the water in the cistern ever cold,
Capped with this lichened, sun-preventing slab.
Of course, no woman with her copper water-bucket
Before the sun rose, comes tripping now.

The second thing was the bread-oven, our communal
'Four', roofed like a bee-skip, dry-stone walled:
Juniper lit with straw for a sudden blaze~
Vine sticks, dogwood, wild-plum wood. The dough
Kneaded house by house in a wooden 'maie', enough
For 'une quinzaine de jours'; the rising whole
Brought to the bake-house in the village centre.

Water splashing communal at source:
Wheat brought to the common fire twice in a moon:
The village stood on pure foundations,
Noë Marty said.

The Buckets

A woman is coming down the lane
In a dark dress with white spots and straw hat
To fetch the potatoes from her stone barn.
She carries two empty buckets.

'Bonjour, Madame Astruc,' we always say~
'Et vous avez raison, le jour est bon!'
Replies. And then again, her buckets full,
Passes the empty house where she was born.

Madame Astruc's House

This nettle-encircled house is home to cats,
Spiders' long nests, abandoned harnesses
And dried-out wine casks in the earth cellar.
An occupied and formal silence hangs on it.
Bleached door, stone steps within, and limping shutter.

But who is the permanent tenant of the place?
At dusk you hear him breathe. No warning given
He floats from Madame Astruc's empty house
Round the big ash-tree to his perch in the barn.
Mice there have no time to be alarmed.

The timing of his long-planned flight takes note
Of darkening Sun, Moon rising in the east.
Though an ash leaf trembles, roof tiles still hot
Lie under air as quiet as his wings.
Unable to speak, my heart says nothing too.

The South Wall

And who is she
against the south wall
of her house
running motionless?

Under her cypress
in blue shade sun
loving
without moving
from his vine?

She Paints

Her material is silence.
She paints the thought

Hidden by trees,
By that bend in the road,

By that cloud.
She sees.

Her dress
Mere substance to her nakedness~

A water colour
On the innocent canvas.

Nora in Occitania

'Occitania'~scrawled on a signpost
By the Haute Serre vines, in the Languedoc.

Two words once made us human, No and Yes.
Audacious No came first: 'Woman will not bow
To brute necessity!' She in a world
Thus humanized got him to open his mouth
At last, and eyes. His Yes was the second human
Word, echoing her No. All words unloosed
Flowed gracefully down to fill the speechless valley.

No made us human in the first sweet place
To plant out vineyards in the land of yes.

Note: Occitania, region of southern France where the ancient 'langue d'oc,
'language of yes', is the vernacular.

Her Deux~Chevaux

Out of the hot valley of the Lot
Her 'deux-chevaux' of duck-egg blue
Billows and sallies like a boat.

Her toes squeezed down
In a shoe of gold on the loose accelerator
We climb, gears groan

Up six stiff bends in the white rock~
Up past the storm-smashed wings
Of the windmill at Cieurac.

Peregrine-like, she cuts
'L'air pur du Causse', hovers
Wings spread. Through the dust on the mirror

Glimpsed valley of the Tréboulou
And watermills. Now
Sets her small nose for home, and 0

Drives my heart in a new gear along
Wrapped in her engine's wild
Sweet, turbulent song.

The Swarm

Between the kitchen door and singing
Tree
The June air thrums and gleams in
Trance
In a rainbow zone of
Innocence
In bliss sunblinded and
Boundless
Nora untouched among the
Bees.

The Thrush

This thrush on the seed-bed tapping for worms.
Her piece of pastel between thumb and finger
Tapping the paper brings up treasure

From memoried ground. Where does beauty
Come from? In the delicious dawn
Purest content to know there is no answer.

Swallows!

Swallows! Why us?
A stream of swallows through the house.
We don't like swallows, that much.

Nora opened the door,
Sun-washed, when one of two
Swallows dived through~
Treading air, trembling
Fluttering against the smoky beam,
Brushing the statice-flowers tied there,
Desiring something, upright
Anxious body curved with the effort of it,
On blue wing,
Like a small brilliant dolphin, or half moon.

Seconds later, out! Blue fire
Wings in a skid under the stone
Lintel above the pine door.
Out, in!
Fluttering against the beam,
Brushing the corn-cobs, circling the dark room.
Swallows, if this continues
We will shut the creaking shutters on you,
And the heavy pine door.

Olivia's Watersnake

In May a watersnake cut ripples in this pool
Now mud—not even comfortable mud
But fissured, with its edges bleached and dried.

Three peasant moons drew down three months of sun:
By day the Sun, by starry night Vega
Stare perpendicularly on Occitania

Scorched to its ancient limestone of the Causse
Where the plough does well to find a foot of earth.
May was a permanent rainbow out of downpour.

Now September breathes harshly in the stricken
Ash leaf, on rigid oak scrub: in his dell
The wild boar at sunrise listens for a light foot-fall.

Tall maize so glossy green in June, now rustles
In the 'autan' wind like grasshoppers,
The meagre cob unfolding from black tassel~

A tattered regiment in desert uniform
Decimated at each corner of the field,
Subjected to some inexplicable defeat.

A diminished peasantry in despair.
Olivia looked into the empty hole, to weep
O, but my watersnake's no longer there!

'La Mère-Chatte'

She herself, the 'mère-chatte' of Piboulède
Suffered perhaps no loss when she got
Crushed flat like that
At Madame Marty's corner of the road
Where the iron crucifix neglected stands~
After a late supper that night.

But her kittens seemed subdued the next morning~
'La Mère' having as milk and mouse provider
Excelled in the village until that moment drear
When panic took her on the roadside verge
Of tall grasses uncut by the cantonnier~
And she sprang shapeless into nothingness at all.

And yet so self-assured and capable a cat
She seems even now to have lost
Little of her forbearing and sufficient
Self among her well brought up kittens.
These race around almost as frolicsome as
When they slept long afternoons between her paws.

The Same Two Swallows?

The same two swallows
As last year?
Standing on the air,
Fluttering at the beam?
They seem
The last two poems left in the world.

By the open door
Fluttering against the dried flowers
Like hummingbirds
On the dark beam,
In windy May
Of 'la lune rousse' ~
With danger of late frosts.
You lift your wings
Not bothering with us.
We make amends.
Come in!

Gaia Hypothesis

A sweetness in the scale of things
Gives to the lizard wings, clear wings.

It is the low that makes the high,
It is the microbe makes the sky.

It is a bird that makes the air,
And a leaf the atmosphere,

As a feather makes the wind
And a seed humankind.

It is some sweetness in the stone
Makes the earth roll on, roll on.

Migrants

Swallows in May to Piboulède,
Swifts, hoopoes.
They go as far as the wind goes.

Eighty million million men have trod
Earth's ancient road.
Where are their lovely bodies, starry eyes?

Two Cypresses

See with what tact, sense of proportion
Marcel Bach's two cypresses grow as one,
Each pliant to the other's mass and shape.

Trees in unplanted woodland do the same,
Arranging space for one another
In mutual aid against the millennial wind,

Lightnings, snowblast, axeman, nuclear winter.
Where the forest makes a mixed society
And maple, scrub-oak, pine and juniper

April by April capture a new fringe
Green inch by inch with leafy ceremony~
When you put your hands up, will they fall in mine?

May Day

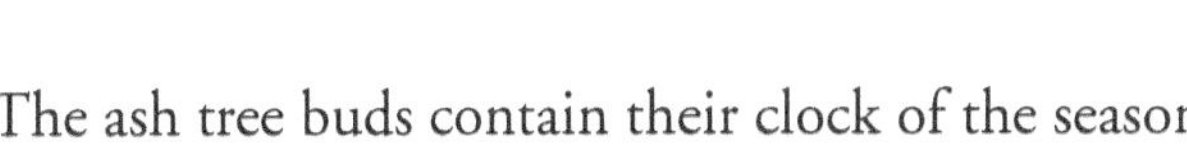

The ash tree buds contain their clock of the season
Spreading out time like dandelion-down.
The black buds point to February

On the low branches, the middle buds to March;
But the leaves bursting on the topmost branches say
Revolution! Yesterday

Was April–but with Winter still
Hiding on the north slope of the long hill.
Today's May Day!

In Limogne Square

——— ∞ ———

The rain falls softly in Limogne square,
Where half the village under thirty umbrellas
Grows quietly together on this Liberation day

To remember 'nos enfants' killed in the wars.
The old watchmaker arrives, with the Resistance banner.
By the bronze cannon, our young deputy mayor:

"Gloire…honneur…la France…justice…mémoire~
Nos fusillés et nos martyrs…" (Here in Limogne
On market day, June I, the 'Das Reich' division

Killed Lambert Puel, age fourteen, and seven
Men in that bloody summer of I944.)
Silence today, and rain.

We stand around. The girl with the trumpet
Running up late, face in a gleam, hair wet,
Strikes out of silence a wobbly Marseillaise~

And under flat black berets and umbrellas
Somewhere in mild hearts Resistance glimmers
In careworn faces, in that ordinary place.

The Town Hall at Montpezat

LIBERTE. EGALITE. FRATERNITE. These words in iron
Letters in the sun above the Mairie at Montpezat.
Words in full sun. The Republic, on calm stone:

Danton. The Commune. Resistance. Revolution.
Well, these words will not get rooted up.
Words germinal: planted, watched for, not in flower yet.

By the hill-presbytery wall, with its view
To the Pyrenees, Celestin Bonesteve (ninety-five,
Blinded in the Guerre de Quatorze, tenth 'hussards')

Slow-marches over the grass of the sheltered Place
To his usual bench in the shade, where we sat: 'Vous êtes
A l'ombre!' he said. Eggshell frail wrist, veined blue,

He gives a clear hand-shake, the lettering of fraternity
In his faceforward greeting, simple soldierly 'salut'.
Liberty and equality by custom graven there.

Three years later, beneath the same shattering sun
We stood in the Place de la Resistance again.
On the Mairie wall, the great letters of the Revolution,

Uncomfortably beautiful,
All had been pulled down as though they'd never been!
(Stuffed into the cellar-lumber very probably,

By the fresh-elected shopkeepers' Conseil.)
In place, an unexceptionable 'HOTEL DE VILLE'
In gold paint shone on a new-scrubbed exterior

All done, no doubt, with a 'remise' on the materials,
The qualified approval of the Leftish mayor
And, as far as permissible, non-union labour.

Down the hill, by the Church of Saint Martin, dragon-slayer,
Stands the plaque to the 'Martyrs de la Résistance'
Against the 'barbarie allemande'. The saint's bones

Dishevelled now with theirs, seem buried that much deeper.
The words of revolution lie still in the cellar.
Celestin, we were told, died earlier this summer.

The Diary

———— ∞ ————

June 29. Great heat.
On this white stone
I sit, listen to Michel's bees
In pleasure pure,
In shade of 'truffier' oak.

'This morning sowed beet-root,' (I write in my notebook).
'Then Nora's statice flowers
And ornamental gourds.'
Smiles Amédée: "Des fantasies!"
Looks at the seeds: "Your beet
Is sown too late." Midi
Arrives: "Et on va faire
La soupe," he says. "Bon appétit!
Allez, au revoir!"

The Dancing Man

Between the sunfire and the new moon~
Up by the high wall of the chateau ruin
Like that since the Revolution~
Aujols village comes to its Fête Saint-Jean.
Here coromel, cabrette, fifre and violon:
Instruments for the songs of Occitan.

Look, every watcher holds a candle up!
Old feet discover step without this light.
A darkhaired and a fairhaired infant girl
Circle the dancers, candle in hand, each calm
As two small moons in solemn counterflow.
Under new stars the human beings glow
In courtesy between the young and old.
The lame man dances and looks beautiful.

Amédée Brugidou

He sings sometimes between the haricot beans
In a sharp hum; then with his pen-knife nicks
The 'gourmand' shoots of tomato or pumpkin,
Following his grandfather's advice.
He remembers the names his grandmother gave to things.

Eighty-four years above the limestone rock
Show him where waters turn, springs tug beneath.
Before he brings his sheep in from the open
Woods of the Causse, he hangs from the plane tree
In the great courtyard at Fournet, shaded at noon,

Buckets of sweet water from the lac.
The sheep crowd gently round, each takes a sip,
Then leaps through the door of its dark house
The bergerie, all dank with dung, smoothed wood,
Stained stone. He lives outside the pages of my book,

Or any book. The moon observes his thin
Handsowings of his own seeds. His hands,
Those massive hands with scarred and nimble thumb,
At sunrise turn to practicalities.
Once, as a boy, he drew the Pyrenees.

The Plane Tree at Fournet

A leaf has fallen from the plane tree,
And the great courtyard at Fournet

Never the same. That amazing tree,
Tallest for miles, an unbroken web

Of branchlet, chiselled leaf, prickled seed-head
In lazy magnitude of sun and shade,

A fountain suspended in green air
Breathed by his sheep, and by the shepherd.

The plane tree levelled now.
Its branches undressed by the dispassionate saw,

Their dimmest shadows ransacked by the sun.
The brindled bole lies stiffly on the stones.

It is mid-September already. His desolate
Dead body small on his daughter's wooden bed.

*Amédée died suddenly at his work at Fournet, on
September 15, 1987. He was 84.*

The Mas De Balmes

Don't say one day
You'll sell
Aujols~
Low house with the high sky
And shadow of the tile upon the wall,
In sunwashed-dry Aujols.
At every syllable you'd have to sell
The thin lip-music her sheep make
As Madame Talou brings them up the hill.
And the gaunt church bell.
The see-saw wash-stones round the lake.
The two cypresses of Marcel Bach.
Your drystone wall, and cavernous well.
In that huge chimney, how could you catch
The juniper sparks
Singing to reach the sooty stars?
By the old, nailed door
Your mirabel in flower?
Behind the house
Ash tree impervious to every wind off the Causse?
Hollyhocks, figs, bay, vine,
Soft rain, diamond sun?
And in the east, at dawn
The cradled, storm-bemoaning Moon?

No Moon

'No moon tonight,' she said,
Her body hidden,
No loving done. Man
Haunted, haunted.

'Your match will not ignite (she said)
Darkness like this:
Fire in the stars, Earth
Moonless, moonless.

The body of the moon (she said)
Hidden like my own.'
The farm dogs quiet tonight.
Dog-fox and vixen.

The Moon is Full

The moon is full
woman

breathes in man
so bright so bright

new moons are nine
now breathes she out

daughter son
more sweet more sweet

on round nipple
her moon is full.

The Bushman's Salutation

It was the moon made woman speak
Mathematical beauty
Original dialogue of three,
To her child and to her man.

Her sun no larger than her moon
Eclipsing fiery magnitudes,
Reduced to her circumference:
Shadow of earth, the moon, the sun

Kaleidoscoping three in one:
Babe his father's furious face:
Her own body in a blaze
Of dark stars burning, loving, turning

1 see you and salute you from afar!
Accept my darkness on your perfect
Moon. Define my fire.
Make my dumb earth speak and sing.

It Was Women

It was women who spoke first
Words in Cromagnon. For a year
Men made no rational answer,

Who had no need of such rarefied means:
With teeth in their hands, or stones.
Men made no words in Cromagnon.

It was she who threw words
In the feminine air: sharp swords
For him to catch, for her sole use.

That night, after supper, "Well, give us a kiss!"
Small-wristed, milk-breasted, her babes
In savage need of eye, arm, polished axe-

She such silk words sexually invented
As made plain to the dumb what was wanted
For the longhouse kitchen, or, "Alone to bed!"

Venez à la soupe, Noë

I was visited last night by the familiar
Person who lives just up the road
Not far away, nor there, but here!
The companionable, forgiving dead
Coming and going with his dog, "la brave bête",
Smoking a maize 'boyard', or drinking en fête
Free of the past as of the future.
At ease in the present, at the tranquil centre.

~But you saw those two hoopoes arrive in the village?
They ran along the lane then flew up flirting together.
~Tomorrow will bring in 'la lune rousse'
Which changes all skies. Frost. Sun. Yes, in those days
We'd harness the oxen under this moon, and plough by Venus!
~"Mais viens à la soupe!" Irène calls.
"Venez. Noë, venez!"

The Autobiography

"I walked a mile from my house in Belut
To marry a girl in Piboulède.

With my horse and my dog, long plough-shaft, two oxen
Ploughed with the sun and ploughed with the moon.

I lie in the earth now, at Saint Hilaire
Under a yew tree, about a mile further."

The Lady of the Presidents of France

We had met her in the Cafe des Amis
In Caussade, eleven or twelve years ago.
Old, but not looking old. Clear shining eyes

She said she'd spent the morning in the rue du Fil
Selling her eggs. Under her chair, a basketful.
Somehow we got talking about this and that

Can you remember what she talked about?
The three wars she'd been in: first her father
Killed somewhere in the 'Quatorze' war;

Then of the last world war, 'les annees noires'
When France herself was taken prisoner.
Her third war the long struggle in Algeria

Against the Resistants of another country.
Her firstborn daughter's death at five years old.
Dark nights recalled, of wartime solitude:

The new baby in her arms all night her one
Happiness in living. Her husband dead.
At the end of this long conversation

She made Nora a present of her unsold eggs,
Placing them safely in our shopping basket.
And before we could thank her properly and say au revoir

(What farewell is for ever, 0 philosopher?)
She told us briskly she had two 'songs' for us.
Other people in the cafe took no notice

But our own hearts began to thump, our ears to burn
At the high beauty of this slight occasion.
They were not songs, there was no melody, yet

Her words seemed made entirely out of music.
The unlikely subject of the market-woman's paean?
From number One to number Ninety-seven

The names, as in a childhood litany,
Of each department of the French Republic.
She spoke each name with such conviction,

Such glee in memory's recall upon the tongue
That people at the tables near began to listen,
Smile, nod their heads, subdue their conversation.

"Ah, here is knowledge~the whole geography and history
Of France from sea to sea, mountain to mountain
From Jura to the Alps, the great Massif Central, the Pyrenees!

Her rivers, land-mass, causse, forests and deep plains
Of France, la France profonde, where Marianne,
Sister of Revolution, wears still her blue white red,

In cornflower bleuet blue, in marguerite, in coquelicot:
Red blood, red wine, red earth, blue sky, white cloud~
The astonishing colours of the First Republic

Calling on mankind, on multitudes oppressed
To stand with France as equal citizens."
This woman at the table, Marianne herself

Discoursing among equals at the Café des Amis.
The overture concluded, her set piece was to come:
She would declare, if we would further listen,

The names and dates of all the presidents of France
From Louis Napoleon Bonaparte, 1848...
By way of Adolphe Thiers, MacMahon, Jules Grévy

To Vincent Auriol, René Coty, Charles de Gaulle,
Alain Poher "par interim", Georges Pompidou, Giscard d'Estaing.
Mighty electoral victories and disasters!

Twelve years or so have come and gone. Nora,
Who is that person with the walking-stick who comes
Stumbling our way, this Monday morning market

In Caussade? "Mais je vous connais bien!" exclaims:
"Vous êtes les gens de Piboulède, je me rappelle~
Mais oui, je me souviens très bien de vous..."

Twelve years have stroked her face with gentle
Fingers, altering her body, changing not at all
Clear eyes, soft voice, forceful expression. The songs again?

"Et pourquoi pas!" sipping a glass of pineapple,
The whole was repeated as before, the music the same,
The rigorous zeal, attention to each syllable.

One name, of course, she added to her litany:
Monsieur Le Président, François Mitterand. The man
For me, she smiled: patriot, man of peace, and a socialist Republican.

Where the Windmill Was

————— ∞ —————

Hill-spring, clear well, small
Stone house with its tiles fallen in.
Everything has lain where it fell.
Unpruned apple, the self-sown quince
And the walnut trees are hers.
The long low wall of stones.
In the high garden above the vines,
Where the windmill was,
Straight at my heart she runs.

For Three Things

For three things I have seen
It is worth confounding death
The unspoken, the unknown
Her face of love on fire,
Moon risen but the sun not set.
The winter stars.

When You Change

When you change direction
Bodily, on a new course veering northerly
I must await the wind from Thessaly
Far out to sea, at dawn~
It may blow southerly.

Dutch Resistance Girl

Artillery makes fun of the church tower,
Bombs blacken bread, turn the milk sour
Among the wounded and the already dead
I saw you turn, to comb your small neat head.

Somewhere near Weert, September 1944

Yuri Alekseyvich Gagarin

"My name is Yuri Alekseyvich Gagarin.
My father was a carpenter,
But I in my eight-and-twentieth year
Russian heaven high was hurled
Above the birch Siberian world."

In the black sky the carpenter's son
Between the raging Sun and mildest Moon
Has seen the blue and brown Earth softly spin.

"Solid and warm the world looks from this height,
No east, no west, no black, no white
But ocean of blue silk without wave anywhere
Turning and turning with the tumbling sphere."

Childlike observer of a planet
Small, serene: whose pearl clouds cover the granite
Furies, napalm fires, nuclear pike and gun,
And man made subject to his own oppression.

The Neap Tide

Listen, I think things will be all right.
I mean, I think we've won (listen
To this quartet of Mozart.)

What victory?

Oh, a curious one,
The very smallest, gentlest, ultimate:
A heart-beat gained
That time we made the bloody-minded
Pause, in the fight against nuclear weapons
Long ago. Yes, that was a loaf
Brought from the oven just in time…

I would love to hear this music once again…

And so you shall, Elizabeth.
Listen again, because I think we've won.
Children are asking questions all over the world;
And out beyond the ribbed mud-flats
Listen, the water has turned.
The dry shells wait.
This morning, in the new weather, the low neap-tide
Has broken against the moon, and along the beach
In racing love returns.

At Churchill's Funeral

His large cat lay curled up on his bed
As Churchill lay eight days dying.
Peter, when someone dies

In Dallas with the bullet in his neck
Or grasping the North Ridge by himself

Or in crowds among miners, soldiers, refugees,
Shoppers, in death camps, demonstrations

Or dies as Churchill, "a statesman by profession"
Or dazed rebel in an African ditch

Shot to pieces with his hands behind his back
Lumumba-like, or Rosa Luxemburg

Dead is that person. Come kings and queens
To the slow funeral at St Paul's,

Let sailors bear that body to the water's edge,
And carry it gently up redeeming Thames.

The Last Post without wavering
Exults and sorrows on the freezing wind.

Schoolday in Man Quang

On Thursday a Vietcong flag was noticed flying

Above the village of Man Quang in South Vietnam:
Skyraider fighter-bombers were sent in,
Destroying the village school and other structures
The bombing mission killed an estimated 34
Schoolchildren, and three adults.

From Man Quang survivors of the raid, not pacified,
Tried to carry the coffins into Da Nang as a protest;
But were held in security by Government forces,
Who made an indemnification over the children's
Bodies; and arrested the parents.

There is no information about lessons in progress
When the school died: civics, a foreign language,
Or 'Practical Subjects'—pottery,
Domestic Science, woodwork, metalwork: in darkness
Burning, dying.

On Thursday a Vietcong flag was noticed flying.

*This incident was reported from Saigon on March 18 and 25, 1965, by
The Times special correspondent.*

The Bridge

No ox, no ox-cart moves in north Viet Nam
By day, in the American daylight~
Sun brings down phosphorus on its high-boned back.

But at night, in the Vietnamese night,
Between village and village boys bring the oxen out
In the water-scented darkness, under a discreet Moon
Whose pity is for the American
Rapist of a proud, neat-breasted, elegant land.

Voices like flowers open all around,
As the women with the ox-carts come to the stream's edge
With the older children, to mend the broken bridge.

Aberfan

Miner has three children,
Wife, and council house.
They love him, he them.
Have nothing else.

Miner put his manhood
Twenty years into the coal:
Longer sweaty hours he worked
Poorer grew they all.

Deeper bloody dug
Coal from the mine:
Higher, higher raised the Tip
Over Aberfan.

Miner had three children:
Two boys, one girl
Learnt from local history
How to die in school.

Coroner, as bound by Law
Issued certificate:
But, "My children have been murdered.
Have you recorded that?"

The school at Aberfan was overwhelmed on October 21, 1966. Almost every schoolchild in Aberfan died that morning. The Chairman of the National Coal Board refused any responsibility for the critically dangerous Tip.

Alice Says No

Alice, in the heat and the boredom
Of a polite summer afternoon
Is almost asleep. Wasp, delirious,
Tugs at her eye-lid, ear-drum.

White Rabbit up-shoots. The adult summons:
Eyes shut Alice
Gropes through sun-meadows, shadows.
Stoops beneath culvert, heavy stones
Through long, cool corridors of stately house,
And ruling class.

"But, how queer everything is today~
Or do I mean this century~
And who in the world am I?
That's the great puzzle!"
(She covers her whole face with her long hair.)

Will Alice hear the sweet and bitter answer~
That two is never two in her real
World: the world that is, and moving, is~
Where a woman and a man is always less
And always more, than what she is, and was
And will be in her moving: he in his turn
To die in a girl's arms, there be born?

Alice, look
Behind this stuffy curtain of illusion
Hung there to separate your childhood from your reason.
See quack historians perform their hysterectomy
On the living body of the people's history.
Attend the authorized versions
Of the English, French, and Russian revolutions.
Or watch the 'constitutional' histories unwind
Through state and 'public' schools into the blind
Caucus-race of university
To feed the armed forces, professions, or the City~
While at prime hours the TV organ booms
Untroubled Anglican, new imperial tunes:

"Who won? Who won?"~paramount question
Of competitive society, market education.
"Prizes! Prizes for all!~
Now take your place on the dole."
Alice, who ran well,
Got back her thimble.

"Who are you? Who are you?" persists the caterpillar.
Alice answers defensively, aware
Of a lucky escape from 1984.
"I'm afraid I don't know, just at this minute…"
But in the Duchess's kitchen regains composure:
"The earth turns on its axis once in 24 hours~
And never on your ugly expectations, uglier fears."
(In the ducal kitchen even such formal logic
Slides into dialectic sense~
Where baby toddles backward into Pig,
Worker is backward driven into Pound and Pence

Redundancy, dismissal by the Board, or Court Sentence.)
"We're all mad here, you know," the Mad Hatter said.
"It's the stupidest tea-party I was ever at,"
Alice replied, "where those who sit and eat
Will neither cook, nor lay the table, nor wash up!"

Alice, you will not meet with truth
However bravely you open your eyes and mouth
While in the enclosed garden it's always 5 o'clock
Strawberry-teas forever of society class-cracked:
Where the gardener's hand and eye embellish
Uselessly the royal, reflected roses in his mind-
Plants without soil, or root, or shoot,
But washed with gold morality and
Painted all the colours of religion and hypocrisy.

Judge: "The knave of Hearts, he stole those tarts-
            And with his life he'll pay!
            For tarts are private property
            And blessed by God, Your Majesty."

King: "Let the jury consider their verdict."

Queen: "No, no! Sentence first, verdict afterwards:
            One Judge does nicely, and one supergrass."

Alice: "Stuff and nonsense!
            The idea of passing sentence first,
            Before the Black Knave has given his defence,
            Before the Silent People have given evidence!"

Queen: "Hold your tongue, Alice!"

Alice: "No! I won't."
"No!" The word of disobedience
Shaped Alice once more to her true human size,
Made her aware of the wasp's insistent noise.
Her dream was over, and the servitude of sleep.
Here, in this meadow, on May Day, and with this
Blade of grass she weaves around her finger
New day begins for Alice
And for England new sisterhood, new anger,
And new justice.

The Field Divided

Ireland unbounded
sold
dismembered
her dancing
word
unremembered.

The lark's wing
wounded
his song
unheeded
my people
dead
the field divided.

Ten Men

Yeats, you must write it once again
Sixty-five Easters on,
How Bobby Sands
With nine friends
A company of ten
Bodily men
Like Cuchulain fought the sea
Of English tyranny.
How in these days
Revolutionary soldiers die in different ways
Instead of drowning choose to die
Naked hungry thirsty to set Ireland free.

"After a Lie, Truth Bursts out!"

After a lie, truth bursts out! *
Ulster to herself unknown
Is Irish yet,
And Irish to the bone

** James Stephens, Dublin, 8 May, 1916*

A Warning

In winter the unregarded sea at Brighton
Neatly expels our daily bits of rubbish
To this high tide mark for bored seagulls
To inspect, and disapprove: an expulsion order
Patiently made out, yet with a warning
From the Moon to the isolated race of Man
Of other bloodier banishments to come.

Twelve Police-Horses

Twelve police-horses in Whitehall,
Bearing grave men with downcast eyes
Lifted no higher than their horses' ears
Listening and unlistening, waiting
(The horses meek, in love with obedience)
For a quiet signal by the Cenotaph:
Blood draining, eyes up now shining
Canter precisely into women, men and children
Chopping them sideways into parsley swathes—
Cutting and turning, cutting and turning,
Explaining with elegance of hoof and truncheon
The ground-rules of the game of State.
"Bastards!" a woman couldn't stop screaming
At minds groomed beautifully as horses' necks
Within oblivious, structured, visored faces.

The Miners' March, 25 February, 1985

The Ram in the Snow

The ram in the snow at Fylingdales
(Picture by Denis Thorpe, for the Guardian)
In Yorkshire, mid-November. Three white balls

On the low horizon. First snow on the moors.
At sunrise the world to its contrived end came.
This ram is steady among the survivors.

He is making the best job of it he can
Though pondering where his next meal's coming from.
It's not easy, keeping up with men.

Summer is due to be replaced next year.
"No animal but man knows death." The ram
Raises his heavy horns, and stands foursquare.

The snow should melt, if it comes on to rain,
And nuclear winter turns to nuclear spring.
No sight, no sound, of melancholy man.

Star Wars

We want it really, the war in the cold stars.
That great Bear! Sirius. Arcturus. Mars.

Pitched from plain Earth, moon-orbiting
Russians make perfected Aliens,
Immaculate targets for homeloving
Americans, our virtues shaped like guns.

How come such talk of nuclear winter, doom?
Star wars, I guess, will not be fought at home.

Odysseus, Lout

Odysseus, lout, sucking up to
Goddesses, lording it over women.
Male chauvinist incorrigible,
Vain, vengeful, humourless, dull
Spinner of complex lies for their own sake,
Ill at ease with the day's truth.
Merciless sacker of cities beyond necessity,
Generous with your companions' lives.
Raconteur. Survivor.
Deliberately Homer
Re-strings his lyre to Woman's waning
Moon. Loosens those gold hexameters
To praise, half-praise the mercenary
Soldier's sly return to Ithaca.

Penelope at mysterious forty
Among her chattering maids in that sea-open,
Sun-filled, salt-sweet chamber
In her high tide of beauty spins, unspins.
Toes neatly spliced in sandals of soft gold
On marble, silk, fleeces of new-born lambs
She lunches with the girls on pomegranate-seeds,
On milky kid, and amber wine. Sometimes alone,
Sometimes with men.

Thug, Odysseus!
Having slaughtered without compunction
Despite their frank and winning, well-phrased pleas
All the young Suitors your competitors
(Boy-bard excepted, spared to sing your praises)
Unconcernedly you arranged to strangle
Those twelve of your wife's maidservants
Who'd had affairs (so said the old nurse spitefully)
With twelve young men you'd just shot arrows through
Using that monstrous bow no man but you
(Hero Odysseus) could bend to string.

Odysseus, you forced those women
Moaning with fear, to wash down with sea-sponges
All that blood from the terrace, clean the tables,
Then collect and put tidy the warm bodies of the killed.
This done, you got Telemachus, your subservient son,
To hang the girls up on their own washing-line
Drawn taut, like "a row of skylarks caught in a net."
The girls' feet, you noticed, for some moments danced.

Odysseus, you should have died at Troy
In flight from Hector. Or in your mocking Horse.
Stayed with those pigs on Circe's isle, Aeaea,
Or in the wounded Cyclop's cave with rams.
And left Penelope to love again in Ithaca,
And every woman choose in the sun her man.

Four Socialist Republics

———— ∞ ————

Four nations form the disunited kingdom:
England, Scotland, Wales. And part of Ireland.

Three are thin. One is fat. England
Is fat through long impoverishment of spirit

Made sick with undigested power, blood:
"A sword and a flay at the king's use"

In Wales, then Scotland. Starving at leisure,
Shooting, raping, then dismembering Ireland

Whose "heart was very damaged indeed,
In pieces," with Mairead Farrell's, in Gibraltar.

Said Alice Green, in 1911,
"The natural union approaches of the Irish nation." *

"That day is far," they say in Dublin
Bars, at drowsy Westminster.

Four socialist republics! The day is here.
Beats at Yeats' "flaming door!"

* 'Irish Nationality', by Alice Stopford Green, London, 1911

Dr Swee Chai Ang's Dream

"Strangely I dreamed of something wonderful~
Of people celebrating in the streets
In Gaza, Rafah, Jabalya and Maghazi.

Stones planted in this way turned into flowers
Of Intifada white and black and green and red
And songs of justice, independence, truth

In voices of the children who have died.
Though I remember Sabra and Chatila,
I dream of the singing Palestinian children."

The Whiteness of the Page

The crows' prints in the snow
Whichever way they go
Alter the universe,

Prepare the way for Man
To make scratches on the Moon
For better or for worse.

The Black Hole in the sky
Is not so far away.
It is the whiteness of the page.

It is what is not.
It is Gloster's eyes put out.
It is Lear's formless rage.

The Land of Pitchipoi

In the land of liberty equality and fraternity
The hand of the clock points now to children's hour.
It was decided on August 15, 1942, to transfer

Three thousand Jewish children in the Occupied Zone
To the transit-camp at Drancy, south of Paris:
Each child decked out in dandelion of yellow star

Above the heart, sewn on his shirt, sewn on her dress,
Her pinafore. The children's ages range from two to twelve.
The youngest ones don't know their names: one proudly claims,

"My name…my name is Pierrot's little brother!"
The unkind rain had washed his name away~
Scribbled in haste and fear on cardboard name-tag.

Drancy is not equipped for children, a camp-attendant said:
Nowhere to put their bundles, bodies, questions, tears~
But wherever are we going to? some older children sobbed.

"This train will take us to the land of Pitchipoi
(A small boy smiled) where all the people will be good to us,
If we do as we are told by the soldiers and police."

These small ones did not understand the height of Grandes
Personnes; could not see beyond the door, behind the engine's
Scream, beyond the blinded windows of the train
That moves without moving through the tunnel of the world
Through the land that has no name, but once was France.
Will the clanking and the shunting never stop?

Of these three thousand children, secured by French police
In sealed freight-wagons for three days and nights,
Not one came back from Land of Pitchipoi. Birkenau-Auschwitz.

*23 August 1990. The facts are related by Ted Morgan in 'An Uncertain
Hour; the French, the Germans, the Jews,* the Barbie Trial, and the City
of Lyon, 1940–45'. Bodley Head, 1990

Crismina and Filismina

Where in the world is East Timor?
Asks Alan Clark, of John Pilger.

Reading John Pilger in the Saturday Guardian,
It seemed I was listening to an unusual question:

Where in the world live the East Timorese?
And, Do you know where Crismina lies, with Rosa, Alisa,

And Filismina? From three western Foreign Secretaries
No word as to where Crismina, with her many sisters, lies.

There has been no clear statement from Douglas Hurd:
Clark, at Defence Procurement, thought the whole thing absurd:

"Foreigners, Pilger, must be allowed their 'civil' wars~
You shouldn't bother so much with their sisters and daughters.

And why persist with the UN 'Illegal Occupation'?
East Timor, so few left alive, hardly ranks as a nation."

Basic common sense, selling arms to Suharto~
Disentangled from Aid—to placate Lynda Chalker.

From a field in East Timor, Pilger answers this question:
He knows indeed where Crismina lies down

With Filismina, Rosa, Alisa, Anita, Adalino, in company
With every member of that glorious peasant family Mendonca.

Who grace with their bodies the same mass grave.
Black crosses shade the hillside here, this riverside grove.

Wooden villages demolished by 'ground-searching' Hawks
Home-built in England, by British Aerospace.

Where in the world is East Timor?
It's just across the road, mate. It's not that far.

Persistent Heaven-Gazing

Religion is
Attendance on Gaia
Earth Mother
Isis.

All new religions are
Male inversions of this mother.
No real loving
Of real creature,

But silly striving
Towards the sun, the empty sky,
Olympus mountain-top, Sinai:
Persistent heaven-gazing.

The Tuzla Tree

A woman hangs
From a small tree,
With her hair tied back
Most carefully.

I am the woman
In that photograph, 
Part of the wood,
Part of the leaf.

My hair is tidy
My legs slim,
My arms hang down
Straight and thin.

I've lost my shoes.
I have no name.
I am the woman
Who was, who was.

Let Tuzla be my name.
Black Thorn. Wild Ash.
I am the woman
Who always is.

Come to me, women
Of Srebrenica,
I call a truce.
I make a peace.

Come with your children
To sort out the quarrel
Of men and religion,
Of men and the nation.

Before we are Muslim
Before we are Christian,
We are always ourselves,
We are always women~

Or I'll hang again
From the Tuzla tree,
With my hair tied back
Most tidily.

*The photograph is by Darko Bandic, in the Guardian, July 15, 1995,
beside Julian Borger's report from Tuzla.*

They Shall Stand up in Ireland

I draw a black
flag round my body
~my babies'
bodies are already
black
burn in my womb
I draw
a black flag round my body
I am instructed to lie down in Ireland

And yet my boys
Richard, Mark, and Jason Quinn
they shall stand up in Ireland
her heart and bone
cold waters and green fields

Their eyes and lips
their eyes
and lips, the noise
and naughtiness all day
my laughing boys

Cold waters and green fields
milk and a green
apple for this morning's breakfast
wash out such fire

cold water and green apples
The measured fire
pushed carefully
through the door
O neighbour neighbour

Wind and sun
and rain, cool rain
endure
endure

Their eyes!

"I am Rosemary Nelson"

Yes, I'm from Lurgan
under Loch Neagh
in County Armagh

My smashed body
on the road
speaks for the truth

again
and again
and again.

Notes on Easter Sunday Morning, 1999

The divine Americans
So early in the Spring
Appearing from the sky
Are already planting bombs
Of great beauty and expense
On the ugly and cheap heads
Of unimportant and degraded
Serbian men and Serbian women
Of no consequence
To the American economy;
And also on the smaller heads
Of their only too degradable
Sons and daughters, and on the even
Less resistant and more unimportant
Heads of their grandsons and granddaughters
All of these are neither friendly nor unfriendly persons
In the military sense, but serve
Without too much screaming
Their appointed role
As collateral damage
Without funeral.

These inconsequential and unlovely
Deaths, a mere addition
To a certain historic crucifixion
But without the bonus

Of any sort of resurrection.
These are the smallest, quietest, most
Perfected deaths.
But we can't now bother
With the incidentals of obscure
Events, of passengers on fire in trains,
Of hospitals and Danube bridges. If the bombs
Seem ineffectual, then bring on
Flowering Cruise Missiles, and all bright
Variants of American technology
Well thought of by our young
Prime Minister, man of new decency
Both ethical and servile,
And in his happy, giggling way,
Murderous as Milosevic.
These sunny April days and
Starry nights, may President and Prime Minister
Bless every mode of Nato bomb
Its lesser and its nuclear mode,
Its Terror arms all brilliant
In the Easter Sun that lightens up
The Millennial New World Order.

The Sea-Shell

Love shall be exchanged for love again,
Sea-shell for sea-shell of exact beauty
Carried everywhere on the world's ocean.

It is the lovely token of humanity
Giving and getting all it has and is.
Money is the obverse of this shell.